The Hearts Live On

Sam Cairns

ISBN 1 901237 31 1

© Sam Cairns 2004

Illustrated by Dave Temple

Printed and Published by TUPS Books,
38 Hutton Close, Crowther Industrial Estate,
Washington, Tyne and Wear NE38 0AH
Tel:0191 4190446

Dedication

This book is dedicated to my father Samuel Newbrook Cairns, a former pit mechanic, who in life caused no-one any harm, yet suffered the agony of seeing himself waste away to a mere skeleton.

Unable to speak towards the last months of his illness, he was tortured by the fact that while his life and dignity drained away before his very eyes, his brain functioned normally.

He knew what he was trying to say, but others around him cried while guessing as to what was trying to be expressed.

To all those who suffer from 'Motor Neurone Disease' my heart goes out to you and your families who suffer with you.

May you live life with the hope that a cure will be found.

Sam Cairns (Jr)

Acknowlegments

I would like to thank the Durham Mechanics' Trust and the Durham Miners' Association for their help in making the publication of this book possible.

When I wrote these poems I wanted to express some of the emotions that I and other miners have experienced over our working lives. Because of the unique working environment experienced by miners I thought that the poems needed some illustration and I would like to thank Dave Temple for providing these. These sketches have added to the poems and will give the non-miner an insight into some aspects of pit life while, no doubt, creating some mixed emotions for the ex-miner.

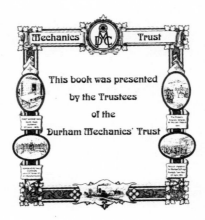

Contents

An Illuminated Darkness

Miners.
Men who daily took on the fight
of defeating Mother Nature
sacrificing sweat
blood
sometimes life itself,
working in conditions that bore
no mercy
no heart
no mother.

In a world of unending darkness
lamps shone a path to follow,
beams of light guiding men to their task
or
to noises
of
creaking timber
falling rocks
danger!

Danger that had to be faced
and
survived in a stinking sewer-like environment
where bait was shared with the flies
and just like the flies
miners lives were spent chasing the light.

Early Rising

2:30 am

Another silent night
is disturbed
by the hammer swinging rapidly from
side to side
smashing against bells that
signal the start of a new day.

Hands
blindly reach out
eager to stop the ringing
the heartless sleep-disturbing ringing
which intrudes upon a dreamy world
where paradise
deletes the need to work for a debt-ridden existence.

In the real world
early morning shift beckons.
The week begins again with
curses
a wash
breakfast
and a visit to the toilet
where yesterdays necessities are dumped into a watery grave
and flushed to oblivion.

Grudgingly, a door is opened
releasing heat into the cold frost filled air,
then closed
relocking in the warmth.

Early morning rising.
The beginning of yet another fore-shift.

Work Bound

3:30am

Crisp virginal snow
is intruded upon as feet walk towards
their bus stopped destination
whereupon
he waits
hands clenched warmingly in pockets,
his uncovered face taut
from the bitter wind attacking each pore.
Boots
stamp hard
crushing snow nearer to an unseen pavement.
Left…right, left…right,
keeping toes from freezing.

A bus approaches
making tracks on the unmarked road.
It stops.
He steps on board
pays his fare
then like the other passengers, his marras,
he sits silently as the bus moves off
pit yard bound
passing houses that seem
to laugh at men up so early in the morning
or
is it night?

On the bus
no-one speaks
no-one moves.
Too tired.
Too god-damn tired.

All Change

3:40am

With clean clothes removed
and inserted into metal wardrobe
nude bodies coldly walk through
short passageways
dividing clean lockers
from dirty
where men ready themselves for
the filth of the mine.

Socks
are smacked onto the stony floor
to soften their starch-like feel.
Jumpers and overalls
are shaken
ridding them of dust and dried-on sweat.
Wellies
are brayed against walls
loosening caked mud that sticks to their treads,
the leftovers of last weeks forgotten shift.

A weary miner dresses
then
dons a helmet
fastens his belt
locks the locker
and slowly moves on to the next stop of his journey
the lamp room
where he, along with other men
goes through the motions of adding
the finishing touches of dressing to go underground.

The Lamp Room

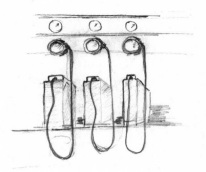

3:55am

In the lamp room
tiredness is temporarily ignored
stored until later
eyes knowing they should be closed
but aware
that, barring any accidents
their time will soon come.

This shift always sees a reversal.
While normal human beings sleep
these eyes must stay awake.
But later while normal eyes are open
these eyes close.

Batteries are guided onto belts
or dropped into pouches.
Cabled lamps are slung over shoulders
or inserted into their slots on battle-scarred helmets.
Self-rescuers, small metal boxes containing filtered masks
giving an hours' protection against smoke,
complete the desired attire for pitwork.

Tokens are unhooked
a silver one to be handed in as the shift starts,
while the brass one is kept until the end.
In-between
should anything go wrong
they will be checked and counted.
Any missing
will be searched for
and identified.
Even the dead must be accounted for!

The Shaft

4:00am

Bells sound
instructing onsetters to allow men
to step into the huge dark decks of the steel rope supported cage.
Tokens are placed into tins.
Fifty helmets are counted into each of the three decks.
Gates are lowered.
One hundred and fifty men patiently wait
then drop into the earth's basement.

In darkness they fall
down a deep black hole
twenty eight feet of space passing by every second.
Only forced air
and the occasional twang of a guide rope can be heard.
Silence is suddenly disturbed by voices
that shout obscenities at the pig responsible
for letting others sample the smells
of last nights ale or curry
or both.

Within this metal cage
men are momentarily trapped
their lives and their families livelihoods
hang by the strength of ropes
tensility of the steely prison-like structure
skills of its makers
and mastery of the winder operator.

They are all trusted
as are the nuts and bolts holding them together.

The Manset

4:05am

The manset idle
while men climb into
its metal compartments
and position backsides
on uncomfortable wooden benches.

Moving on
some men sleep, resting bored and weary eyes.
Others lazily talk
discussing the weekends news
or sexploits.

Small groups play cards
the stakes being high.
Mars Bars are gambled
as wheels roll on endless parallel rails
guiding a way through countless miles of darkness
arched in a never ending lane of girders.

With the destination reached
men alight.
The sounds of 'mealy mealy' are aimed at
card school losers who try to hide or disguise
their embarrassment.

Overmen and deputies assign work-places to needy men
so begins the long enduring walk
to where their task awaits
tasks that must be accomplished
to provide a living.

All Uphill

4:35am

Nine hundred metres of hill beckons
its'strength sapping gradient
inviting guests
to amble
or chance their health and hurry.

To amble is to lose money.
To hurry is to gain.

In what feels like a lifetime of sweating
and panting
the uneven stony surface is conquered
but no flag stands at the top of this hill
just earth,
earth that waits to be mined
devoured by machines
the metallic monsters that constantly add
yet more distance to tomorrows walk.

An Early Bait Stop

4:50 am

With the hill thankfully behind
and heavy coats hung on knotty timber
men rest
and cool their sweat while
drinking water-bottled water
flasky tea
and eating paper-wrapped sandwiches.

Three men sit in a heading
a forty metre advanced tunnel
with only one entry
the one and only way in
but more importantly,
the one and only way out!

In unison the men rise
and ready themselves to commence battle with mother nature.

Now the work begins.

Forgotten Time

5:10am

And so to work,
the heading men set about their task.

A huge dirty white tank-like machine stands
waiting under covered ground
its turret outstretched
aimed towards a wall of coal
and stone.
Picks impatiently stand by
ready to bite a passage through the enemy...Earth!

While two men prepare necessities
the machine operator crosses two handles
setting picks in gear.
A tap is turned on
causing water to shoot through jets in the cutting head
ready to fight its dusty foe.
A button is pulled
sending power to the mechanical heart
of this ground eating beast.
The cutting head rotates
spinning picks and water in a circular direction.
Operating handles are pushed down
ordering fixtures to obey commands.
Tracks, the machines' metal wheels
comply by biting into the floor and slowly moving forward
pushing tungsten pointed picks into the land.

All time is forgotten now.

Think only of the job
and of course...its dangers!

The Dust

Picks continuously turn
noisily chewing coal that stands before them
their prey cascading to a dirty floor
where rivers of black diamonds are gathered by paddles
that circle the machine.
Contents are dumped onto an awaiting conveyor belt
which in turn drops its load to another
then another and another
until eventually the light of day is reached.

Underground
black dust fades away
as a band of stone is encountered.
Picks take smaller bites
travelling slower across their controlled line.
The noise grows louder.
White dust billows all around
defeating the airbag currently battling to keep clear the vicinity.

The operator, he stands
wearing a mask and goggles
his eyes straining to see through the density.
Assisted by two machine mounted lights
and his trusty cap lamp
he knowingly guesses where the cutting head is
realising that hitting a previously set girder
would result in an affect that could be
catastrophic
for himself
but more importantly…for others.

Ever Watchful

As the final piece of reachable stone
is ploughed up by the machines' spade
and paddled off to oblivion
two metres of land stands
exposed
naked
waiting to be supported.

Eyes look.
Ears listen,
watchful
for signs of any rocks that might fall.

Without warning
a stone drops
just a small stone that could do no harm
but
are there bigger ones to follow?

Men probe the area
making sure they are relatively safe.
How can they know?
Only what is seen can be checked.
What about the unseen?

Safe Ground

Heavy rust-covered girders are carried forward
through claggy mud
that tries to hold onto its intruder.

With the help of the machine
united with mens courage
skills
and strength
each girder is set
then fastened together with metal plates
coupled with nuts and bolts.
Once again, mens lives
are trusted with nuts and bolts.

Timber is positioned
tightened down
wedging the roadway into place
helping to alleviate the risk of falling rocks
that could injure
maim
or
kill!

Not all ground can be covered
but as in all pitwork
certain hazards come with the job
and must be accepted
but hopefully
avoided.

The Faceline

Away from the heading stands a faceline
a five foot high two hundred metre long wall of coal.

Above and below
is stone
that serves as a floor and roof
or in bad conditions…a hindrance.

On hands and knees, men crawl
over steel chocks
their supports from the earth overhead.

Knee pads are constantly invaded by particles of sharp stone
pressing against flesh
biting and gnawing a way through layers of clothing and skin
causing discomfort
and pain.

Men follow the double-headed cutting machine
that powerfully rumbles on
noisily aiming for its goal
the facelines end
the main gate or
tail gate.
One gate to the other equals a cut.
Each cut equals more money
but more work
more crawling and bending
more hurriedly dodging rocks
as well as water that drips from the roof
each drip helping soak its target
be it man, or machine.
It doesn't matter which.
The water doesn't care.

Production

The leading drum of picks rampage
through the faceline coal
uncaringly raping its victim
in a destructive fashion.

Coal teems onto the endless panzer
the metal conveyor with countless steel bars noisily scraping
onward
carrying their loads
to the point where
they empty themselves
onto another chained conveyor
before returning to gather more coal
more money
more profit.

A Piece of Paper

Faults occur
not only in strata
but also in machinery.

Men wait impatiently for their repair
so that they can get on with the job
instead of having to sit freezing in the cold windy tunnel.

One miner takes a piece of possible toilet paper
from inside his helmet
and a small pencil out of a dusty pocket.
He writes down thoughts
and memories
of a fathers tale of yesteryear's pitwork
where technology was not then introduced.

Words written
he reads it
studies it
admires it
then returns it back to the straps of his helmet
where it will stay
in case of emergencies.
No toilets down the pit
no paper…unless hidden.

A Miner's Tale Hidden in a Son's Helmet

My eyes they see
yet
without my lamp
I am blind in this darkness that surrounds me
in this man-made hole called
a mine
dug with picks and shovels
supported by props and straps
rock packs keeping apart roof from the floor.

Men sweat
their skin reeking of dirt
that clings to their body.

Salty water drops steadily from cracks in the roof
onto aching limbs.
A drop lands in a miner's eye as he timbers up his ground.
His dirty wet hand tries
to wipe away the stinging acidy water
which burns and tempts a prodding finger
to spread more pain
onto a face that expresses its displeasure.

Curses are spoken
words being choice.

I share the light
of a colleague's lamp.
Together
we support the roof
making safer our place of work
and together we support...
the mine.

Our Threatened Land

With the machine's wounds mended
it ploughs on once more
through coal that acts
as a temporary inconvenience.

Men follow
fulfilling their required task.

In the heading
the men steal another yard.

The pit is working.
Production is at full swing
but elsewhere
in one of the countless roadways
danger has showed itself in more than just
a threat.

Trapped

Using bare hands
men frantically shift rocks of all sizes
trying to forget
the screams they'd heard
amidst the loud rumble preceding the fall.
They rummage like rats trying to escape the doom of
an approaching predator...
death being the predator.

Through the carnage
dead friends are pulled out
bodies crushed to a pulp
limbs twisted and broken
distorted in positions impossible to a living form.

Grown men cry. Some vomit.

The same men who daily laugh at near misses
and curse the stones and rocks
that find their targets
the men who simply shrug off the bruises
and blood that seeps a path along a dusty limb,
they cry.
Shocked at the sights just witnessed
tears drip down coaly faces
as friends are carried out
no more to be seen.

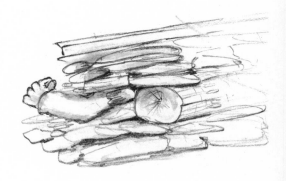

So What!

A pit
and all it contains
must always
repeat always
be respected.
yet
it
does not respect man.

So what!
if a man is killed.
A pit has no mother.

So what!
if children never see their father again
or wives become widows
or mothers will be childless.

A pit
has no heart
no feelings
nor sympathy for those whose lives it destroys.

Stop Everything!

Dead colleagues
will soon fade into memories
joining the ever-growing list of
seven day wonders
forgotten
except in passing conversation.
"Remember Bill? Remember Ted? Both killed last Thursday.
I wonder how much my wages are this week?"

Again
men assisted machines continue to strip the land
not caring about mother earth
thinking only of more money.

Within the walls of warm lit offices
away from the mines' thick strata
power argues against power
representatives of both the coal board
and union
demanding they win
each one explaining their case for a better future
for men
        for the industry
                for themselves.
Who do you believe?

Over tannoys below
the cabled intercoms,
orders are given
"Stop all machines and
            get the hell out!"

The strike…has begun!

The Miners' Hall

With all seats taken
and standing room at a premium
miners share rumours of striking reasons.

The rumble of voices cease
as their leader enters
walking on stage, proud
high and mighty
telling them that confrontation
is unavoidable.
The government now becomes the enemy...mentally
but it's the Police who they will be fighting against...physically.

Through doors too small for mass departure
men squeeze their way outside
and make for
individual destinations
homes
pubs
clubs
each man thinking his own thoughts about
events to follow.

Some look forward to it
others do not care.

Some secretly wonder
if maybe they should take any notice of their so called leaders.
After all
unions don't pay the wages
so who is right?
the bosses?
or the union?

1984 — The Year of the Picket Lines

Months into the strike
the chorus of "Scab! Scab! Scab!"
echoes through the air
that fills the spectatored streets.

Abuse is hurled
as are bricks and bottles
at meshed windows of buses carrying
strike breakers
blacklegs
escorted by dozens of Police vans
each scab claiming numerous officers
as his own personal bodyguard.

Chants of "Zulu! Zulu!" are followed
by hundreds of pickets surging towards the occupied buses
the battle buses.
Police lines take the strain
the thin blue line
thickened
with a mass of uniforms invited from other establishments.

Bodies press against each other
against what seems like
an immovable force.
Lungs gasp for air.
Legs dodge or take the blows of boots.
Ribs cry out for an ease to the contest
silently screaming.

Men are glad when the push subsides.

Trouble on the Lines

A milk float that stopped nearby
was raped by uncountable hands
who then hurled their capture
at an innocent line of Policemen
whose task was simply to
guard the gate,
yet they found themselves
evading bottles.

Glass smashed against whatever it hit.
Walls and pavements were automatically covered
in milk splattered slivers
mixed with blood
from those unable to avoid
the torrent of hatred thrown at them.

Police reinforcements arrive
immediately attacking whoever obstructs their path.
No questions are asked.
Those who wear no uniform
are classed as
foe.
Neighbourly bystanders are no longer treat as bystanders.

Truncheons are rammed into stomachs
or aimed at unprotected heads.
Fingers, trying to cover skulls
are uncaringly broken
as are hearts
many many hearts.

The Aftermath

Thousands of men tear into each other
having no respect
for uniform
age
or in some cases
sex.

Horses obey their bridled commands
and charge through rows of men
and women
who gallantly fight
for their jobs
their future
their lives.

Hooves crush bones
trampling on exposed heads
arms
legs
anything that stands
or lies
in their way.

The unconscious
remain unconscious.

Others
continue the battle.
Separate fights and beatings
take place at numerous sites of the blood stained land.

The aftermath reveals
no winners
just losers
both sides injured in body…and soul
all hatred forgotten as the day ends
inviting men to return home
to brag to friends
show off captured souvenirs
mend wounds
or simply cry on sympathetic shoulders
trying to forget
how man can treat fellow man
with a hatred that attempts to destroy
life!

Is It Really Worth It?

In an unfair world
pickets cannot win.
They can be punched
kicked
and beaten by policemen who at the end of the day
return home.
Yet
if a picket reverses the situation
he will be arrested
thrown into a van
hidden from the mechanical witnesses,
the cameras seeking pictures that can reveal all...If allowed to.

He is then handcuffed
then held until a court appearance
where in most cases he will
repeat WILL
be found guilty
then receive whatever punishment
befits the crime.
In his cell
he might wonder if it's all really worth it
fighting for a job
that can kill without mercy or compassion.

Four grey walls encompass him
furnished with a bench and open plan toilet.
Is it really worth the embarrassment?

One-time Friends

Hopes of a return to work
are dashed once more
as one side holds out a peaceful hand
for the other to reject.

More and more men lose patience and confidence.
They succumb to a normal life
where wages are earned by
working.
Ignoring threats, they return.

Weeks later, their children smile
as pocket money is once again given
food is plentiful
and bills are paid.

Through the meshed windows of the escorted bus
they see despair
and hatred on the faces of
one time friends
who still loyally suffer
along with their families standing on the dwindling picket lines
singing the customary chorus of
"Scab! Scab! Bastard Scab!"

Who cares?

The Strike Ends

The strike ends
along with countless friendships
divided communities
neighbour against neighbour
and endless talking behind backs.

Children are warned
as to who
or who not to play with.

Kids who were once
nice kids
good kids
are now
"Their kids".

Should they be the ones to suffer the indignity
of parental hatred?
Have they not suffered enough?
Was Christmas not emptier than the rest
food more sparse
sweets rationed or donated by others
and pocket money a rarity?

Were they not frightened
when a brick smashed through a window
or a Policeman knocked on the door?

In the end
was the strike for our children's sake
so that they might have a future
or was it a test of strength
for
the powers that be?

The Return

Marching behind lodge banners
men enter the now unprotected gates
singing
"We're miners united...We'll never be defeated"

With heads proudly held high
each man keeps his heart felt thoughts hidden
from the media led population
who look on through netted windows.

But who has won?
Us?
Them?
Each side claim victory
but for what?
Will we get back our missed wages?
Will they reclaim lost production?
Will the Police regain their respect?

At the end of it all
                 did anybody bloody well win?

Back to Work Down The Pit

Even the pit has changed.
The structure is still the same
but
the atmosphere is different.

All the mice have died
starved of scraps for a year.
Girders have gathered more rust.
Timber has grown foisty growths.
The air is dense
with hatred and animosity.

Bosses now have the upper hand
ruling with fear.
If after refusing to obey an order
who would back you now if you walked out?

Work harder
make up for lost time.
Basically…Do as you are told.
If you don't like it, there is always one alternative
You could always look for another job!

Thoughts of Another Job

Who would employ you now?
Are you not now classed as a trouble maker?
For a year
twelve whole months
you defied management
giving your loyalty to a union.
Will the union employ you if other managers do not?

Maybe thoughts of another job
should be instantly dismissed.
Think only of the future
as a miner
with enough coal to mine until your retirement age.
At least that's what the bosses say.

Coal is reckoned to be plentiful
so why all the rumours about pit closures?

Pit Closures

Announced pit closures
headline the news.
Your pit is included.
Are you surprised?
Didn't you already know that one day
you'd be unemployed?

But what, you ask, of the coal that remains?
Well! What of it?
It's no longer your concern.
People only burn the stuff anyway!

Another Fight

Meetings are held
pressure-groups formed
to try and change the minds of those in power,
those that don't care
about men who over the years have
given their all
broken their hearts
as well as backs
and have sweated blood
and in some cases
lost limbs
or died for their country.

Their loss isn't cared for
or remembered by a government
which considered looking after
themselves…and their own kind
the money people of our supposedly classless land.

To them, the working class are scum
who must take pay cuts
and work more hours
to earn an annual wage
that money people can earn in one week
one day
one hour!

So it's back to the fight once more
again to keep pits open
for a living…
or is it a hell?

Final Days

Underground
the last day has arrived
bringing with it a sombre death like atmosphere
which surrounds every roadway
every junction
every faceline
every heading
every heart.

Production work ceases.
Men lazily see off their final day.

Remaining coal
is reclaimed by mother nature.
Machines are powerless to perform.

Only the outward journey remains
and it's all downhill.

For the Last Time

For the last time
men
leave their place of work
ride the underground manset
walk the windy road to the shaft
ascend in the cage
hear the sound of forced air
hand tokens to the banksmen
replace self-rescuers and lamps
take off dirty smelly clothes
shower in the block where so much dirt is washed away
and where so many jokes were played
on unsuspecting soapy-eyed mates.

For the last time
men
change at their lockers
making themselves presentable for the outside world
and for the very last time
men
walk out the gates
never to return
surplus…
to requirements.

Jobless

Many times during despised past days
men have cursed the next shift
having moaned and groaned
about the times they should be asleep
instead of having to work down a dusty black unhealthy hole
expressing comments about the dangers, wages and conditions.

Yet
many now sit
bored with their jobless lives
wishing the old days
could magically return.

Maybe in dreams
perhaps they could break into a world
that offered hope of work
then again…maybe not.
Reality must be faced.
There is no such thing as a dream-world!

Yesterday's Ghosts

Pits have died
taking with them
communities
to graveyards full of past times
times that saw men
with bait-boxes stuffed into pockets
trudge through snow, hail and
a mixture of seasons.
to help keep this great land warm
and lit.

They were unrespected
taken for granted
by those who knew nothing about pitwork
but enjoyed its privileges
the fires
the lights.

Now those men are gone
forever lost
their jobs replaced
by the ghosts
of
yesterdays workforce.

Memories

The mighty and powerful
who control our land and
our destiny
might be able to make decisions
then flatten
where once was stood
a mine.

With one stroke of a pen
they can
and do
take away men's livelihoods
our childrens future
and wages that families depended on,
but one thing they cannot control
the one thing that remains untouchable
out of reach of their power driven fingers
is...
our memories.

Video Thoughts

Switch on ones brain
fast forward
stop
play
nothing there…no visions displayed…everything blank
rewind
search for pictures of yesteryear
pause
think about the view
good time? Bad time?
unpause and rewind further
play
remember happy days
when work was plentiful
and the future looked promising.

Eject
then ask yourself
what can the brain tape for tomorrow?

Remember the Forgotten

In the shadow of a mine
stands a graveyard
where lie
countless boxes of memories
in a field full of friends
over-shadowed by the spirits
of the men who
laughed
cried
lived
and died
thus becoming
another box of memories
in a field full of friends.

Epilogue

It's a sad fact that mining will never be the same again.

A handful of pits still exist, but for how long? Who knows? Not you. Not me. Not the workers, the governmental pawns in the financial game of chess.

In the past, pits, supposedly unprofitable, closed due to government statistics which were used to try to brainwash the British public into believing that imported coal was cheaper so more economical for the Country.

Did the brains of the powerful not realise that once we became dependent on yet another import, prices would rise, and rise, and will continue to do so.

Did those same brains also never stop to think of the knock-on effect of putting thousands of miners out of work? Did they actually know how many other industries it affected? Even if coal was cheaper, did they sit down and work out the true costs in paying redundancies, future state benefits and all the other costs associated with people being out of work? Did they care?

Or did they simply pass on the power to someone else, then live out their luxurious worry-free lifestyles, while countless affected families struggled to cope.

Many people over the years have accused miners of having too strong a hold on the country. Would those same people prefer another country to have that supposed hold?

Mining in most parts of Britain is now dead, buried, filed away in the historical sections of libraries throughout the land. Many people, especially the youth of today and tomorrow, will not know what a pit is. Mining will live on only in the minds of those who did their bit in an industry which provided coal for a nation in all times of need.

Miners are resilient. Many have done what they do best — adapted to their changed circumstances. Jobs have been sought and gained. New skills have been learned and put into practice.

Miners whose health was destroyed by the many diseases associated with mining and those whose bodies were worn out by sheer hard work or crippled in accidents, have not fared so well. But whatever has been their fate, one thing is certain — they will never forget that part of their life spent as a miner. It is in their hearts, and no matter what, their hearts will live on!